The Baby Cow &
Other Children's Poems

Written by Jenna Feitelberg
Ilustrated by Maddy Moore

Briley & Baxter Publications | Plymouth, Massachusetts

ISBN: 978-1-954819-21-4

Book Design: Stacy O'Halloran

This book is dedicated to Elisia and Emma,
you both are the sunshine in my life,
and to Jason for believing in me,
and always pushing me to reach for the stars.

The Puppy

"Do you have 20 dollars?"
My puppy asked me one day.
"What for?" I asked in a curious way.

"Well I need to go to the dry cleaners,"
my puppy explained matter-of-factly.
"What for?" I asked again.
"Why the dry cleaners exactly?"

"Well to clean my coat of course,"
answered back my puppy.
"What's wrong with the bathtub?"
I asked quite abruptly.

"I can't use the bathtub."
He walked over to show me.
And when I looked at his dog tag,
it read "Dry Clean Only."

Monster In The Closet

There's a monster in my closet,
and I don't know what to do.
He smells really bad,
and he's chewing on my shoe.

I tried to get him out by offering him some food.
He didn't seem to want it.
In fact, he acted pretty rude.

I offered to read him a book before he went on his way.
He put his nose in the air and said,
"I don't want to hear a book today."

I offered to let him keep my shoe,
but he didn't want that at all.
I told him, "You can't live in my closet
because the closet is too small!!"

He took that as an invitation.
He did not leave, but instead,
I'm now sleeping on the floor,
and the monster's in my bed.

Baby Sister

I tried to feed my baby sister,
but she pressed her lips real tight.
I made a choo choo sound,
and her face lit up with delight.

I went closer with the spoon,
and she closed her lips once more.
The spoon just bounced right off
them and landed on the floor.

I tried doing a silly dance.
This made her giggle and smile.
I tell you this whole routine
went on for quite a while.

Then she picked up her bowl.
Yay, she's going to eat! I thought.
But instead she raised the bowl into the air
and dumped it on her head.

The Baby Cow

I went up to a baby cow.
It was so very cute.
I said, "hi!" to the baby cow,
and at first, the cow was mute.

Then all of a sudden,
I heard the cow say, "Baaaahhhh."
I looked at the cow and thought,
well that is quite bizarre.

I responded "moo" to the cow,
and she didn't make a peep.
This baby cow thinks
she's a baby sheep!

I looked over at the berry and asked,
"Why are you so blue?"
"Well being blue is just something
that blueberries do."

I wondered if they changed their name to
orangeberry, would that be better.
They would never have to be blue again.
They would shine in sunny weather.

But then the blueberry explained right that very day,
"Just because it's my color
doesn't mean I feel a certain way.
In fact, you can't judge who I am
by the color of my skin.
Just because I'm the color blue
does not mean I'm feeling blue within."

"Oh, so being blue on the outside
does not indicate the berry that you are?"
"No, my friend,
you cannot judge a berry by looking from afar."
The blueberry gave me insight.
I felt so happy that day.
I guess every berry is unique in a very special way.

The Tree

Why do you wear your winter coat in the summer,
and in the winter, you are bare?
That doesn't make any sense!
Aren't you cold sitting over there?

And then at the end of summer you
throw all your clothes on the floor. My
mom and dad have to go to the yard and
rake and rake some more.

You should really clean your mess!
I have to clean up my room, for goodness sake!
I will go inside and get you a rake!

Swing From The Moon

Yesterday I decided
to swing from the moon.
At first, it was hard
because there was no moon at noon.
But then the night time came,
and I got my rope with a tassel.
It was difficult to hook the moon.
I mean it was really quite a hassle.
But hook it I did,
and I swung away.
Now, how do I get down
because soon it will be the day?